PRAISE FOR "A WORK IN PROGRESS"

"I first want to commend Ashley on such a challenging project. I titled this review, 'A "Gutsy" Move' because of the nature of its content and her lack of experience, but nonetheless, knowledge that Ashley has captured in the conversation of her writing.

Marriage is a much disciplined lifestyle between two individuals who have decided to become one for the rest of their lives. So many of us have experienced, at one point or the other in our own lives, a time when we came into a marriage without being legally married, just to later divorce without having to endure the judicial breakup between lawyers and many controlled plans made by the courts. Surely the nastiness and the heartache which accompanies this rigorous process without the fundamental understanding of a real marriage continues to be an easy cycle of defeat that many non-believers and believers go through, causing so many good relationships to end because of fear and not wanting to be Godly-committed. This book provides a scriptural tutorial for guidance and direction.

Perhaps others continue to endure the long cold wait of desiring marriage, but in your singleness, you continue to fail by marrying over and over again to those who want covenant with you. In addition, many others fail

by never getting to know God and what His desires are for marriage, knowing what His word says. Truly, Ashley is making a gutsy move by sharing this and much more in her book. Ashley's understanding is intriguing, and her knowledge of the scriptures clearly brings a level of wisdom that illuminates the original purpose for man and woman since the inception of time.

With this being the first but challenging project for her, I can assure you that we, the readers, will cherish many future materials published by this young anointed, up-and-coming author. I'm personally excited about what God is doing in Ashley's life, and I'm looking forward to seeing great things from her in the many days to come. She truly is a gem and rare diamond in the Kingdom of God. Watch out book world... Here she comes!

– **Apostle Lamont A. Hill,** Overseer & Teacher
Kingdom Exousia Ministries, Int'l – San Antonio, TX

- - - - -

"The title of prophetess is a mere testament of the faith, obedience and desire you have for the Father in those late midnight hours, waiting patiently, pondering, in tears, the depths of wisdom being given you—always seeking understanding, singing songs from the very

depths of your spirit, storms and waves in a whirlwind of creative mystery by the Holy Spirit brought together to whisper truth into the heart of women all over the world; silencing the threats of doubt, deceit and hurt from all the men who refuse to be who they are called to be. Ash, you have raised a standard as bearer, writing a refreshing yet riveting look into the truth of WOMAN, giving a diagnosis with clear prophetic vision. May these words educate in the uniqueness of all humility to unlock secrets of Genesis 2:23&24 KJV: "And Adam said, this is now bone of my bones, and flesh of my flesh: she shall be called Woman, because she was taken out of man. ²⁴ Therefore shall a man leave his father and his mother, and shall cleave unto his wife: and they shall be one flesh."

– **Paul L. Patterson**, Author
The Apostle's Anointing

- - - - -

"A Work in Progess is a masterpiece that should be in every church library, counselors' bookshelf, and in every hand of any woman or man who would like to get married. It's often said that you can't lead anyone to a place that you have not been. Don't look at this book as

small because the advice and the stories in this book are big.

Ashley is taking you through every aspect of your life and teaching you how the bad can lead to good when you embrace all of the challenges, emotions and feelings you have inside. It doesn't matter if you're married, divorced or single. Ashley will take you through life as a spiritually married woman, a hurt woman, a divorced woman, and as a single woman, but, at the end of this book, you will realize that not only did Ashley take you through every emotion, she also added God's Word to help you through.

This book is powerful and, I, Laticia Nicole of #SpeakLife, encourage men and women to allow the words to teach, guide, renew and rebuke you as you realize our lives aren't fairytales made in heaven. If it were so, I wouldn't have a reason to read this book. The first chapter had my attention and kept it until the end of the book. Wives, know your role!"

– **La'Ticia Nicole,** Bestselling Author

#SpeakLife: Your Tongue Has the Power of Life and Death (Vol. 1)

A work in PROGRESS

Exploring Biblical Perspectives
on Marriage, Divorce and Singleness

Ashley Smith

A Work in Progress
Copyright © 2015 Ashley Smith

All rights reserved. No part of this book may be reproduced, distributed or transmitted in any form by any means, graphics, electronics, or mechanical, including photocopy, recording, taping, or by any information storage or retrieval system, without permission in writing from the publisher, except in the case of reprints in the context of reviews, quotes, or references.

Scriptures marked NIV are taken from the Holy Bible, *New International Version*®, NIV®. Copyright © 1973, 1978, 1984, 2011 by Biblica, Inc.™ All rights reserved.

Scriptures marked NKJV are taken from the Holy Bible, *New King James Version*®, NKJV®. Copyright © 1982 by Thomas Nelson. All rights reserved.

Published by: Purposely Created Publishing Group™

Printed in the United States of America

ISBN: 0-942-83828-X
ISBN-13: 978-1-942-83828-9

Special discounts are available on bulk quantity purchases by book clubs, associations and special interest groups. For details email: Sales@PublishYourGift.com or call (888) 949-6228.

For more information, log onto
www.PublishYourGift.com

DEDICATION

I dedicate this book to everyone who desires to love and be loved. May you experience the true authentic love of the Father, whose love never fails.

TABLE OF CONTENTS

Dedication		ix
Acknowledgements		xi
Foreword		xv
Introduction		xvii
From Ashes 2 Life: My Testimony		1
Part 1	Wives	15
Part 2	Unequally Yoked Marriages	29
Part 3	Divorced	35
Part 4	Unmarried Women	43
Part 5	Singleness	51
Part 6	Words of Wisdom	57
About the Author		63

ACKNOWLEDGEMENTS

First and foremost, I thank my God, my Lord and Savior Jesus Christ, for without Him I would not be, and this book would not have been possible. This book solely came by inspiration of the Holy Spirit. I pray that each person who reads this book will be blessed beyond measure and will gain something that can be applied to their life.

I give honor to my mother and best friend, Linda and my father(s): Darryl and Terry. Thank you for who you have been in my life and the values and lessons you taught me that I carry with me today.

To my grandma, Linda, Sister Linda and Brother Darryl II, I love you all too. Thanks for being my support system.

I bless God for my babies, my big boys, Anthony and Va'Sean. You boys are my inspiration, the reason I

A Work in Progress

smile, the reason I choose each day to move forward in faith. I love you both more than words can say.

Also, I thank the many women who shared their testimony and words of wisdom with me to share with the world. I pray God's blessing upon all of you and your households.

Most of all, I thank the one woman who has been with me every step of the way, my own personal editor and prayer warrior, Mrs. Stephanie Grier Williams. I love and appreciate you more than you know. May God continue to bless the work of your hands and increase you all the more.

I thank Lady Sarah Grace for blessing my book with a foreword and my Apostolic Father, Apostle Lamont Hill, Mrs. La'Ticia Nicole, and my brother in the gospel, Min. Paul Patterson, for reviewing and offering constructive criticism of my book.

I thank my godmother, Mrs. Gloria Smith, for always being there with words of wisdom and thought-provoking questions along the way.

And last but not least, I thank all of my brothers and sisters in Christ who have kept me lifted in prayer throughout this journey; the prayers of the righteous surely do availeth much.

Ashley Smith

I also want to leave a space for whomever I failed to mention: I truly thank you, _____, for all that you have done along the way to help me birth this God-given vision. Without you, I could not have done so. God bless you and remember Jesus loves you!

XIV

FOREWORD

FOREWORD BY SARAH GRACE

A Work in Progress, brings a very necessary message to those looking to find God's will in the area of relationships. Right relationships have tremendous power, especially those of a romantic nature, and it is of the utmost importance that we learn how to govern our lives with right standards in them so power is worked for the good.

Ashley shares from the scriptures and also from her heart, bringing a balanced viewpoint that is both Biblical and practical. She helps us see the beauty and sanctity of relationships built on a right foundation, and she also helps us see the deception of thinking that we can force a blessing on something that God hasn't ordained. All the while, she weaves in the timeless message of God's gracious ability to take our ashes and give us beauty when we have to surrender it all to Him and start over again.

Though the world says "what you don't know can't hurt you," the Bible teaches otherwise. In all our getting, we are to get an understanding in every aspect of our lives. This book will help you understand the purpose and power of marriage, divorce and singleness and share wisdom and direction through scriptural content and Ashley's personal testimony. It is sure to bring hope and healing to women who feel that their hearts have been broken for the last time and help them to avoid that heartbreak by applying the principles shared in this book.

Sarah Grace

Author of *The Woman with the Issue of Love*

INTRODUCTION

The word of God says in Genesis 2:18 (AMP) that, *"it is not good (sufficient, satisfactory) that man should be alone. I will make him a helper meet (suitable, adapted and complementary) for him."* As women, we were all created from the rib of the man God chose especially for us, but before we meet or are even ready for our mate, we are often led astray. We also tend to fall into the hands of the counterfeit sent by the enemy to distract us from reaching the will, purpose and plan that God intends for our lives.

The definition of counterfeit is: *made in exact imitation of something valuable or important with the intention to deceive or defraud.* For a woman, this deception is usually in the form of a man who exemplifies everything she has ever desired in a companion. He looks good on the outside and is perfect on paper. A dream come true until he gets her hooked through sexual and emotional soul ties, even marriage. Then he, usually unknowingly, carries out the enemy's plan to steal, kill and destroy her and/or her destiny.

A Work in Progress

Many times, the reason for this deception is the hidden pain within our hearts that causes us to go searching for the love we never received as a child. That love search causes many of us to settle for the first thing that *looks* like love. At least for me that was the case. I, myself, have never been married naturally, but I was married six years spiritually. I fell in love without truly knowing love. Without knowing love, I could not see that I was not really receiving the same measure of love I was giving out, so I was settling for an illusion of love and did not even know it. Through sin and my ignorance to the truth, the enemy was destroying my spirit, killing my joy and stealing my peace. The enemy had stolen my identity, which caused me to not understand who I was or understand my worth.

It was not until June of 2011, when God divinely interrupted life as I knew it that my eyes opened to the truth. That's when I realized that I had been living a lie that would do nothing but end in my destruction if I did not turn from my sinful ways and surrender completely to Him. At that time, I had been living with the fairytale in my head that every girl dreamt of. I had hope that happily ever after would come soon. I believed that as long as I continued to be a good person who treated others as I wanted to be treated, stand by my man and work hard, it would all pay off. That may work when you are living a holy life, but my life was anything but that. I was fornicating, having children out of wedlock, partying, cursing, cheating, stealing and lying to get by. Deep down, I wanted to live right because I knew there was a better life for me. Plus, I had been taught better than that growing up. I wanted to get married, finish school and be a good example for my children. I believed that I had found the ONE and all we had to do was get right with God.

We began to take steps towards God to change together, but God had other plans that required us to be apart. The ending of that relationship brought forth a new life, one that introduced me to the lover of my soul.

Ashley

FROM ASHES 2 LIFE

MY TESTIMONY

It has been said that God doesn't call the qualified, He qualifies the called. This is a portion of my testimony that has given me the wisdom and experience needed to write a book such as this. As stated in the introduction, I have never been legally married, but in the eyes of God, I was married for six years to one man. And like the woman at Jacob's well, I have married a few other men as well. There are so many women out here that are loving and living a lie. In my six-year relationship, I strived to be all my man needed and wanted in a woman because he loved me unlike any other man in my life. He looked me in my eyes and promised me that he would never leave, no matter what happened, and I believed him.

A Work in Progress

For him, I gave my all. I strongly believed in standing by my man and proudly lived by the motto, "If you don't feed your man, someone else will," and I meant that in every way possible. There wasn't much I wouldn't do to keep him happy. He would tell people that I treated him like a king, even when he didn't deserve it. I made sure there was always a hot meal on the table, the house was clean, and he could always count on me to open my legs whenever he was in the mood. I was his number one supporter. Whether he was doing his rap thing, working as a bouncer in a strip club, selling pounds of "green" or a brick of "white," I was there. Yes, I was scared, nervous and paranoid all of the time because although I had strayed away from God, the morals that had been instilled inside of me growing up had never left. That still, small voice still whispered to me and caused me to feel conviction. Times were always hard, but we were determined to make it no matter what it took. It was he and I against the world. That determination to make it by any means necessary caused us to be put in desperate situations, which resulted in us doing things that we said we'd never do.

The very first thing I should have paid attention to was the fact that, at the beginning, he told me over and over again that I wasn't his type; he didn't usually date girls who looked like me. I wasn't a redbone with nice long hair and an hourglass shape. I was the opposite. I had the long hair, but I was dark skinned, smaller around the bust and slender with little junk in the trunk. Unlike the women he was used to, material things didn't faze me. They were nice to have, but they were not a requirement, for I was pleased by the simpler things. He was opposed to my looks but attracted to my heart and what he thought he could get out of me. I had dealt with a low self-image concerning my complexion most of my life up until that point, so to hear it again just gave me the fuel I needed to prove him wrong. On the outside, I may not have been his type, but on the inside, I was convinced that I had all he would ever need in a woman. I set out every day to prove him wrong, yet his constant reminder of this caused me to always feel inadequate.

As time went on, he continued to proclaim that I wasn't his type, yet we went on to pursue a relationship. In response to his declaration, I would tell him, "You're my man, you just don't know it yet." For the first time in my life, I saw someone/something I wanted and I went after it. Looking back, that was an example of God showing me how my words shaped my life. In a few months, we were living together without an official title because he wasn't big on titles and just wanted to "go with the flow."

A Work in Progress

So we settled in together, and I, in the meantime, did all I knew to keep him happy. I was committed to living peacefully by any and all means. For one, I felt lucky to have snagged someone like him. Since he constantly reminded me that I wasn't his type, I knew I had to step up my game in order to keep him. In my mind, I had to prove that I was worthy of having someone like him to love me. He was handsome, tall, had a nice athletic frame, worked two jobs, lived alone (even if it was in the projects), had his own car, only one baby mama, came from a loving family and was respectful. He had a rough side to him, knew just about everybody and was respected by every man, no matter what side of town we were on. He was who men wanted to be and who all the women wanted to be with. Loving his family was important, but I soon came to find out that his definition of what it means to be a man was distorted. In all actuality, I didn't know the definition either. My natural father hadn't been a part of my life since I was about three years old, so there was no one for me to compare him to. I didn't have a father figure who was involved in my life enough to step in and warn me to stay away from him. No one told me that the love I so desperately needed could only be found in God.

In that first year, I fell into what came naturally to me. I lived in submission to that man as a wife would to her husband, including letting him make decisions for us. Soon I found myself being the only one holding a job, and this continued through the rest of our relationship. I would work for months, even up to a year once, without any help. We were always struggling financially, and everything I had became his. He knew how much money I had and when my paydays fell. He was in control of a lot more of my life than he should have been. Two years into the relationship, we welcomed our first son. I fell in love at first sight for the first time ever and really enjoyed my new title. That still wasn't enough to make him want to go get a job though, so I went back to work after six weeks and put my son in childcare because going to the gym was more important to his father than staying home and caring for his son or going out and looking for a job. By the time my son was three months old, I was working a second job. At least three days a week, my baby was spending about 12-14 hours at daycare. It was as if I was living as a single mother. Yet and still, I tried not to complain too much. I would let things go on until I became too stressed out to handle it. I believed in family, and I hated confrontation. There was nothing I wanted more than for my family to stay together, even if it meant that I'd have to shoulder most of the responsibility.

I hadn't seen my birth father in over ten years, and my mother divorced my stepfather when I was sixteen;

A Work in Progress

in turn, he divorced us children also. Again, there was no male figure for me to compare him to. No one told me that I didn't have to settle for this type of lifestyle or define what a man's role was. Nor was there anyone there to hold me accountable to the confession I had made at the age of eleven stating that Jesus Christ was my Lord and Savior. I was just all about keeping my family together and now that I had one child, any other children I had would have to be by the same man. To me, that was more important than being married. I spent too many years wondering what my father looked like and looking in the mirror trying to see who I resembled on my mother's side, and I didn't want my child(ren) to go through that. It was so bad I remember asking my mother, at the age of nine, if I was adopted. You see, I didn't know I was beautiful and fearfully and wonderfully made. I didn't know I was more priceless than rubies. No one told me that a real man loves God more than he loves you, so I spent at least six and a half years giving my all to someone who did not even deserve it because I felt as if I didn't deserve it.

We welcomed another baby boy the next year. By this time, things were starting to change. He was still in between jobs, and I went back to school to try and better us because I could not see us getting out of this cycle of financial stress unless I did something. I was also getting tired of being the girlfriend. Yes, he

Ashley Smith

promised me forever, and we talked about our dreams for the future. Through those talks, God used me to help him find his true passion and calling. We began to talk more about marriage, and he picked out a ring that he wanted to go back and get. I had my finger sized, and we just wanted to get on the right track. An opportunity of a lifetime became available to him that would require him to travel for extended periods at a time, and I just couldn't stand in the way of it, so when he asked me if I'd be okay with him going, I said yes. Saying no would have possibly cost him his life, by either death or incarceration.

He left for a few months and would send a little money here and there, and we went to visit a time or two. When he came back, we discussed relocating to begin a new life where he could be closer and continue the same work and really begin to pursue his passion. We began praying together each night that the will of God would be done in our lives. Little did we know, the will of God would turn things upside down.

Once again, he was to go back to work out of town. This time he packed up all of his belongings, and me and the boys were to follow two months later. We said our goodbyes, and I did all I could to swallow the lump in my throat and keep a dry eye until he turned the corner. I continued going to school and working, raising our babies as best as I could in between. A few weeks went by and he called me saying that he was about to get baptized. I cried and thanked God. I wanted nothing more than for him to get it together so we could do things the right way because whatever he did, I would stand behind him and line up accordingly. I also cried because I should have been there. To me, this was something that your family should be able to witness. Nevertheless, he was giving his life to Christ, so after voicing that, I let it go and again gave God praise. Over the next few weeks, he would call and share all that he was learning about God and the Bible. I was fascinated and excited. We would listen to gospel music together over the phone or follow each other by way of social media and listen to what the other shared. We'd also purchase the same books.

In the meantime, I had prepared to leave my job and make my way with my boys in tow across the states to reunite our family. A week before my last day at work, his namesake, and my soon-to-be stepson, was badly injured in a so-called child prank. He was hospitalized for about two weeks, so I stood in his father's place. Every day, after working a twelve-hour shift, and on my days off, I would be there in his hospital room, along with the boy's mother and her family. The other mother and I didn't really know each other too well as I always made it a point to stay out of things concerning their son. And our boy's father would keep me shielded from her due to their own strained relationship. So even though I didn't know what to expect, I went anyway because he and I were a unit. Unfortunately, he couldn't make it back here for a week, so I continued my visits. Four days before my man was to arrive in town, he called me and said that when he got there we needed to talk. Immediately I wanted to know what for, but he assured me it was nothing bad.

The day before he was due in town, I cooked his favorite meal because I would be working all day on his arrival. After work, the boys and I met him at the hospital. We were all excited to see him, and I noticed that he had a glow about him. He looked cleaner than usual and his skin was brighter, but I was also concerned about how he was doing seeing his son in that condition. As we sat in the hospital room, and it came time to change the bandages, I knew that this would be the time that would be hardest on him. Just as I thought, seeing the bandages undone broke him down. I went to comfort him, but I felt a wall up between us that hadn't been there before. Though he barely hugged me, I kept quiet about it.

Three days went by, and he stayed at the hospital the whole time. I couldn't understand why he hadn't come home yet. So on my day off, he finally left the hospital to go with the boys and I. We went grocery shopping, he came to the house and ate, took a nap and then finally said he was ready to talk. We went into our room and he began to tell me about this vision he called a revelation from God. In short, God showed him people and events that would take place in his life if he obeyed. I couldn't see where I fit into this whole vision until he uttered the words, "*I gotta let you go.*" Those words hit me so hard. It shattered my heart. I didn't understand. How was this possible? This could not be what God said! I was good for him. I bent over backwards to give this man a peaceful life, treated him like a king and gave everything I had plus some! In the midst of my confusion, I remember looking up through my tears and saying, "God, I guess I'm supposed to thank you 'cause you said that we are supposed to thank you no matter what the circumstance, so I thank You, I guess." What I didn't realize is that according to man and the world's standards, I was good, ideal and one whom others should compare their woman to. But I've come to know that nothing is good if God is not in it, not even me.

Chaos broke out, and even his family was shocked. They loved me and didn't believe he had heard right. I couldn't tell my family yet because I didn't want to hear my mother say, "I told you so." Hearing him speak those words made me want to give up on everything,

Ashley Smith

but when my then three year old looked at me and asked why I was crying, I knew then that I had to muster up some strength to continue moving forward. Those days following were rough. I remember that very night as I lay down to sleep, there was a heavy weight on my chest. I cried myself to sleep, praying and begging God to relieve the pressure I felt on my heart. I couldn't eat for about three days. I remember sitting on my bed a couple nights after that, doing my hair for church. Because of all the crying, not eating and barely sleeping, I passed out. My body was exhausted because I wasn't taking care of myself and had fallen into a state of depression. Even though I wanted to call off from work, I went anyway to keep my mind off of things. I made frequent trips to the restroom to hide my sudden outbursts of tears from my co-workers. At one point, I even contemplated suicide. I was driving my boys to daycare, and I thought of just speeding up and crashing into the brick wall up ahead. I remember thinking, "Now I know why people kill themselves," but immediately following that, I remembered that I'd go to hell. Hell is one place I didn't want to go, and I definitely did not want to take my children's lives along with mine.

With all of the confusion and depression going on, I was seeking God for answers because He was the only one who could explain all of this to me. God made sure

A Work in Progress

I felt His presence every day for at least a month straight. Jesus carried me through that. Despite how devastating this situation was, I received hope through the promise that accompanied the revelation. God said that if I turned and submitted to Him, He would lift me up. I cried out to God over and over again, but was convinced I could not hear His voice. Eventually I told my family, packed up my children and moved back to my birthplace to be near my family who had since moved back home. I didn't know what to do with my life because I was so confused and had given so much of myself away in this dead-end relationship that I didn't have anything left for myself.

I continued to seek God, diving into His Word and praying for healing. I got baptized again and came to know God in a whole new way. He showed me why He had to break apart my relationship and explained who I was in Christ Jesus. You see, God is a jealous God. No one can come before Him. I had made that man my idol, putting him in the place of God. I loved him more than even myself. God showed me the difference between real love and showed me examples from this prior relationship that was everything but love. God told me, "You deserve better than that. I gave my only Son for YOU." He showed me that we had done things backwards and that he wouldn't bless our sin. We had been illegally married, living in fornication and having children out of wedlock. That, among other things, wasn't bringing anything but curses upon our lives. It is because of God's grace that He saved me from a life of destruction and misery by the dissipation of this relationship. While I knew He was real and still living, I never thought that it was possible to have a relationship with Him as you would a person.

The relationship with my ex ended four years ago, and God has moved in leaps and bounds in my life. I now know my true identity and am no longer lost in confusion. Never would I have imagined that I'd be where I am today. It is only by His grace that I have been brought from ashes to life and am now a virtuous woman and mother, a multiple business owner, a published author, a minister of the gospel of Jesus Christ, an emerging prophetess and more. The scripture that I would use to define the greatest lesson I have learned from that relationship would be, *"And thou shalt love the Lord thy God with all thy heart, and with all thy soul, and with all thy mind, and with all thy strength: this is the first commandment"* Mark 12:30 KJV. Loving God with all that you have in you will causes you to never put anyone or anything before Him. Truly loving God means that you don't intentionally sin against Him and you do your best to keep His commandments. In loving God, you are free to not only love others, but also to love and honor yourself first. I have not yet arrived and can honestly admit that I have a ways to go, but I'd rather be a work in progress than forever lost in a world of sin.

1

WIVES

I (Bride/Groom name), take you (Groom/Bride name), to be my lawfully wedded (wife/husband), to have and to hold from this day forward, for better or for worse, for richer, for poorer, in sickness and in health, to love and to cherish; from this day forward until death do us part.

For many of you, these are the traditional vows that you pledged to your mate before God, family and friends. These vows are not just promises spoken to your mate; they are promises to God. It has been said that God loves us through others, and I couldn't agree more. Just think of the relationship between a parent and their child, best known as *storge*.

A Work in Progress

Storge is a Greek word that expresses the kind of love a parent naturally feels for their child(ren). It is unconditional, meaning no matter what your child does, you still love them. They can break your heart, disappoint you, push you away and just all out go against everything you have ever taught them. Nonetheless, you still love them. That is one of the ways that God loves us. The best way to define the love that God has for us as His children is known as *agape*, defined as an unconditional love that sees beyond the outer surface and accepts the recipient for whom he/she is, regardless of their flaws, shortcomings or faults. This is the same love that Jesus Christ our Lord and Savior demonstrated on the cross. It is also the same love that God commanded through Jesus that we have for others in Mark, chapter twelve.

God holds you each and every day in the palm of His hand. He is with you through your best times and your worst. He is there when your finances are overflowing and when you can't even find two dimes to rub together. He is there when you are down and out and when you can run without fainting. God loved you and cherished you before you were even formed in your mother's womb. By carrying out these vows, you are representing the physical manifestation of God's agape love, and His love never fails.

Ashley Smith

WIVES: KNOW YOUR ROLE

When you get married, you take two whole individuals and merge them into one. The husband becomes the head, and the wife acts as the body. Everything about you comes together. Becoming one is something that happens both naturally and spiritually. In the natural, your name, income, credit history, taxes, bank accounts, and more all combine, and you are seen as one unit. In the spirit realm, all of your spirits, sins, blessings and curses intertwine. God designed marriage as a part of His perfect plan for mankind.

> *"Therefore shall a man leave his father and his mother, and shall cleave unto his wife: and they shall be one flesh" (Genesis 2:24 KJV)*

It was in (Genesis 1:26-27; 2:7) that God formed Adam out of the dust of the ground and breathed into his nostrils the breath of life. He then placed Adam into his dwelling place, his home, the Garden of Eden. God told Adam what his role and purpose was here on Earth. He gave Adam kingship (dominion) over the Earth, told him to subdue (bring it under cultivation) it, be fruitful, multiply and replenish the Earth. In other words God said, "This is your home. Work it and take care of it; you'll be in charge of all living things."

A Work in Progress

Then came a helper, whom Adam called woman because she was built from a piece (a rib) taken from the side of man, and he gave her the name Eve because she would be the mother of all the living. They were created equally to carry out the work of God in this natural world. Adam was purposed to be the head (leader) because he was created first and was physically stronger. Order was set upon creation: God, Man, then WoMan. God created man and gave him the vision, the word: God blessed them and said to them, *"Be fruitful and increase in number; fill the earth and subdue it. Rule over the fish in the sea and the birds in the sky and over every living creature that moves on the ground."* Then God said, *"I give you every seed-bearing plant on the face of the whole earth and every tree that has fruit with seed in it. They will be yours for food. And to all the beasts of the earth and all the birds in the sky and all the creatures that move along the ground—everything that has the breath of life in it—I give every green plant for food"* Genesis 1:28-30.

In turn, Adam turned around and relayed the word to Eve. She was made to be Adam's helpmeet—a companion to assist or help, to surround, protect, to aid, to gird. The rib in the human body and every living creature is in place to surround and protect the vital organs and provide structure and support for the whole body. So if you, the helpmeet, who was made out of the rib of your husband, are not in place, injury or major damage can occur to your marriage body. That is why it is important to always be in position.

Somewhere along the way there was a disconnect between man and God. Adam was not exercising his authority of dominion. He was supposed to be watching over and protecting his home, the garden. Due to the fact that Adam was out of order, there was an invasion in their home. The enemy, also known as the serpent, slid into the garden and deceived Eve.

The enemy appealed to Eve using lust to get her to go against what God had told Adam. Let us be reminded of (1 John 2:15-17 KJV), *"Love not the world, neither the things that are in the world. If any man love the world, the love of the Father is not in him. For all that is in the world, the lust of the flesh, and the lust of the eyes, and the pride of life, is not of the Father, but is of the world. And the world passeth away, and the lust thereof: but he that doeth the will of God abideth for ever."* The serpent told her to *look* and see that the fruit was beautiful and it looked good to eat. The serpent convinced her that the fruit would make her "all-knowing and full of wisdom" just *like* God. All she would have to do is eat a piece of fruit from the tree of knowledge of good and evil. He convinced her that she would not die but live, which was the direct opposite of what God had told Adam.

The enemy attacked their body when he deceived Eve and proceeded to take out the head (Adam) once the forbidden fruit had been partaken of by them both. Not only were their eyes opened, but their spirits died. The partaking of that piece of fruit was not just a means of opening the blinded eye. It was a direct attack on God by the enemy. He found a way to get the one thing God hated the most (sin) inside the thing He loved the most (mankind). This act caused Adam and Eve to die spiritually and begin the process of dying naturally. Soon after, God came looking for them and found them hiding their naked shame. At that time, they confessed their sin to Him. He then punished them by casting them out of the Garden of Eden and passing judgment upon them.

As a wife/helpmeet and woman, it is very imperative that you understand your role. Your role is determined by your purpose. As stated previously, the woman was created to be a companion, to assist or help, surround, protect, aid and gird. Let's break all of these words down so that we can have a better understanding of what they mean:

- <u>Companion</u>: A person employed to assist, live with, or travel with another.

- Assist: To give help or support to, especially as a subordinate or supplement; aid.

- Help: To give assistance to; aid. To contribute to the furtherance of; promote. To give relief to. To change for the better; improve.

- Surround: To extend on all sides of simultaneously; encircle.

- Protect: To keep from being damaged, attacked, stolen, or injured; guard.

- Aid: The act or result of helping; assistance.

- Gird: To encircle with a belt or band. To surround. To equip or endow. To prepare.

The word "helpmeet," broken down in Hebrew, is defined as this: Hebrew word *ezer*, meaning to aid or help. Hebrew word *azar* is a prime root, meaning to surround (i.e., protect or aid: help, succor). Genesis adds that the primary idea lies in girding, surrounding, hence defending. Meet Hebrew word *kenegdo* means corresponding to, counterpart to, equal to matching.

The key to being a successful helpmeet lies in this scripture: *"And whatsoever ye do, do it heartily, as to the Lord, and not unto men"* (Colossians 3:23). When you are being a helpmeet to your husband, you are doing so out of reverence to God. You are to serve the man that God has placed in your life as the head of your household cheerfully and not begrudgingly. Doing so pleases God and allows you and your household to be in order with Him. Also, serving or being in submission to your husband does not mean that you are to be walked on or treated as a child with no say so. Husband and wife are brought together in marriage by God for a kingdom agenda.

Marriage helps build the Kingdom of God. You are working together to ensure that the vision, plan or assignment God has given your husband for your family is accomplished. But submission and serving does not just apply to the woman. The word says that, *"The head of every man is Christ; and the head of the woman is the man; and the head of Christ is God"* (1 Corinthians 11:3 KJV). Therefore, we are all submitting to and serving someone as the head of our lives. It's all about trusting the Spirit of Christ in your husband and respecting him as a man, leader and individual. The Bible teaches women to, above all, respect (reverence, submit, adapt to) your husband, and that men must love their wives as they love themselves and as Christ loves the church, which is unconditional and unfailing.

Submission has gotten such a bad reputation over the years. It is mostly due to the fact that men have abused it, and both men and women do not understand what it means. The dictionary's definition of submit is to yield or surrender (oneself) to the will or authority of another; to give in to the authority, power, or desires of another; to allow oneself to be subjected to something. In the case of marriage, the definition I have found to be most favorable is to be under the care/covering of the person God has ordained just for you. To be under someone's care means that they take care of you, lead you, guide you, protect you, provide for you, love you and pray with and for you. Submitting to your husband does not mean he will have complete control over everything you say and or do. You do not have to be subject to abuse whether physically, mentally or verbally. God does not condone that type of behavior.

> *"Every wise woman buildeth her house: but the foolish plucketh it down with her hands." (Proverbs 14:1 KJV)*

As a woman, most of the time, the stability of the house depends on you. The woman usually sets the atmosphere in the home. Being a nurturer, the love and energy you give to your family makes a tremendous impact. You are the one who feeds, educates, trains, develops and cultivates the members of your family.

A Work in Progress

They look to you for love, approval and assurance—both children and husband. You have the ability, along with your husband, to make your home filled with peace, love and laughter. Think back to your own childhood or to your own children, remember when you fell off your bike and skinned your knee? You ran crying to your mommy and she cleaned it, put a bandage on it, kissed it and made it all better. Your kiss, your love makes it all better. We also know that when mama is mad or upset, the whole house feels it. Your attitude and approach will either help build your household up strongly, or weaken and tear it apart.

> *"You should clothe yourselves instead with the beauty that comes from within, the unfading beauty of a gentle and quiet spirit, which is so precious to God." (1 Peter 3:4)*

A gentle and quiet spirit is not one that never has anything to say or has to take on this role of weakness. It is best described as one who is not overbearing, pushy (bossy), stubborn, selfish-minded or quick to react, but to *respond* out of love. Reacting is usually done out of the flesh without thinking. Responding, however, is often followed by a moment of thought or prayer, and takes into account all that has been said or done. When it comes to dealing with your husband, it is important to always address him in a respectful, loving manner. I believe it was Steve Harvey who said, "There is a king and a fool inside of every man, and the one you address is the one who will respond." As his partner, you are to speak words of encouragement and praise. There will be times when constructive criticism is needed, but it must come from a place of love in order to be effective. Your choice of words and your tone of voice is very critical in how you communicate things to your husband. Remember, as (Proverbs 16:24) says, *"Pleasant words are as an honeycomb, sweet to the soul, and health to the bones."*

(Proverbs 15:1) says that *"A soft answer turns away wrath but a harsh word stirs up anger."* You do not have to tear him down when trying to make a point by attacking his manhood, which would include, but is not limited to, his ability to provide, his intelligence, his leadership skills or anything else that would tear him down. It is important to talk to or with him and not at him. The Bible says that it's *"Better to live in a desert than with a quarrelsome and nagging wife"* (Proverbs 21:19 NIV).

Oftentimes we, as women, can speak to our husbands in the same tone that we use for our children when trying to get our point across. The thing to

A Work in Progress

remember is, we all only have one mother, and, as his wife, he needs you to be just that—his wife, lover and friend. If it's something that cannot be agreed upon, then it is your obligation to take it to God in prayer.

There of course are times when a soft answer is not your first response. Marriage is a work in progress and a labor of love. It's not something you float through. It is a journey taken by two people who absolutely refuse to give up on each other, no matter what storms they have to weather along the way. That being said, there will be times when your mouth may cause you to sin. You may say something out of anger, or even be oblivious of the offense. In these situations, you will have to humble yourself and apologize. It is always wise to pray first when these circumstances arise. Ask God to give you the grace to humble yourself and the words to speak that will cause the situation to be dissolved. You may even be right in the situation, but the fact that your husband was offended is enough to warrant an apology.

This all applies if you are on the other end as well. Lots of times we get into arguments, and all we want to do is go to God and tell on our spouse. Do we ever stop to think that it may be us who needs to be fixed? Maybe you took the situation the wrong way. Or maybe, you made a bigger deal out of it than it really was. You could be just misunderstanding your spouse's point of view. Either way, someone has to be the one to make amends. *"In your anger do not sin": Do not let the sun go down while you are still angry*, (Ephesians 4:26 NIV).

Jesus is the one leading your husband, and sometimes that is who it'll take to convince him to change his mind, decisions or pathway. Although he is covering you as the head of your household, it is your job as his wife and helpmeet to cover him with prayer at all times. Your family depends on your prayers. The woman described in (Proverbs 31:15) rose up during the night to get her meat (spiritual food). That spiritual food is praying, fasting, reading and studying your word. God created man (us) to be in fellowship with Him. He longs to spend time with us. He has so much to say to us, and it is in that time that you are drawn closer to God through His spirit.

Most of the time women spend so much of their day taking care of everyone else that they leave themselves out. It is very important to have time to yourself, not just alone with God but also to take care of you. Have a day of pampering, or half a day, whatever is doable for you and your family's schedule. Get a new hairstyle, get a mani-pedi (or do your own if it's not in your budget to get it done professionally), hang out with some friends. Have a girl's night out or meet for lunch and shopping on a Saturday. Go to the library and get lost in a good book. Go for a walk on a trail and just marvel at the creations of the Father. Take a nap! There are plenty of things you can do and enjoy by yourself.

It is also good to allow your husband time alone by himself or with friends. Time apart every now and then will be good for your relationship. It gives you a chance to miss each other and something else to talk about besides the kids and household responsibilities. Also, the most important thing to remember to do is spend quality time alone together. It is so very necessary to continue to date each other. You don't even have to spend money to do so. Put the kids to bed early and turn on some music and dance in the living room. Watch a movie together with popcorn and soda. Cook dinner together. Go for an evening walk. Get up early and watch the sun rise together. Stay up late and talk about everything under the sun. Just continue getting to know each other and keep the passion burning between you two.

2

UNEQUALLY YOKED MARRIAGES

"Can two walk together, except they be agreed?"
(Amos 3:3 KJV)

Have you ever been in the shoe store and tried on one high heel and walked over to a mirror to see how it looked? I'm sure the walk was a little unsteady, pushing up to balance on the high heel and coming back down on the flat foot. If I asked you to run could you do so? As I picture that run, I see myself falling or twisting an ankle. If you and your husband are not on one accord, it's going to be hard to move forward in the same way that it would be if walking with one heel on.

A Work in Progress

The Bible tells us in (2 Corinthians 6:14) not to be unequally yoked with unbelievers. One of the definitions of the word yoke is "to join, link or unite." When you become saved, that means you have made the choice to make Christ the head of your life. The word also says that *"...the head of every man is Christ and the head of the woman is man..."* (1 Corinthians 11:3). So if you are saved but your head is not, how will you effectively serve Christ? Part of submitting your life to Christ means that you no longer live according to the world's standards. You must live a set apart life in which you apply the word of the Bible to your life.

Applying the word of God in your life shows that you are in agreement with His commands. Keeping His commands will cause blessings to be bestowed upon your whole household as the Lord promises blessings for obedience (Deuteronomy 28:1-14). Your head is supposed to lead you in the right direction, and if, for example, you are submitting to Christ but your husband is submitting to the world, how can you grow together as opposed to growing apart? It is also much easier to grow as a Christian when you have support.

In an unequally yoked marriage, there will be a continual battle. The enemy will use your husband to go against everything you seek to do in the name of Jesus. You may want to spend time with God, studying your word, meditating or praying, and your husband, who doesn't share in your faith, will most likely look at those things as a waste of time. He may feel as if you should be using your time for things he views as more productive. While it will surely make you feel frustrated if done repeatedly, you have to remember that your first ministry is to be to your family. The family unit is made up of your husband and yourself. Your children are blessings to the family. You must keep in mind that the spirit in your unsaved husband is doing its job by keeping you away from anything concerning God, so you may have to get your alone time in with God while your husband is working, sleeping, or on your break time at work. That way you can feed your spirit without interruption. You'll also find that the unsaved will know and try to use the word of God against you in order to get their way. For example, your husband may ask you to do something while you are trying to have quiet time with God. You may respond by suggesting he do it himself or wait until you are done, and his reply might be, "Well I know the Bible says that you are supposed to obey your husband! Somebody is being a hypocrite."

As tough as it may be, try not to get too upset because when the devil tempted Jesus, he tried using the word of God against Him. But how can you use the Word against the Word? Jesus responded with, "It is written..." followed by scripture three times until the enemy went away for a season. In your situation, it may best serve you to begin quietly praying the Word to keep your flesh from rising up or to bring it back down. You can respond with the Word, but darkness does not comprehend light (John 1:5). Even though he may know some of the word, it is mostly used for his own selfish reasons. When someone refuses to give their life to Christ, they are denying their belief in who He is. How can you use God's Word and not believe in Him or His Son? That is why the Bible was written for the church, the saints, and the "aints." The aints do not understand it, so they use it to meet their own agendas whenever they feel it is necessary.

> *"And if a woman has a husband who is not a believer and he is willing to live with her, she must not divorce him. For the unbelieving husband has been sanctified through his wife, and the unbelieving wife has been sanctified through her believing husband." (1 Corinthians 7:13-14 NIV)*

There are some women who become saved *after* they have married their husbands. If your husband does not become saved as well, you are now in an unequally yoked marriage. Although you have given your life to

Christ and are now committed to serving Him, you must also still respect your husband as the head. Your husband still remains first after God. You are still to love, honor and support your husband unless he asks you to do something that goes against the Word of God. *"Wives, in the same way submit yourselves to your own husbands so that, if any of them do not believe the word, they may be won over without words by the behavior of their wives"* (1 Peter 3:1, NIV).

Your husband is watching you and really paying attention to every change that occurs in you now that you have confessed Jesus Christ as your Lord and Savior. It is almost like his salvation depends on you because you are the closest person to him, and if he sees you changing for the better and can see the Spirit of God in you as you are taken from faith to faith and glory to glory, he will want what you have. (Acts 16:31 NIV) says, *"They replied, 'Believe in the Lord Jesus, and you will be saved--you and your household."* So continue to treat him as the king he has been destined to become and let your walk with God win him over. Your new way of living will have more of an effect on him than your words ever will.

"Life and death are in the power of the tongue..." (Proverbs 18:21 KJV)

A Work in Progress

Be careful of the words you speak about your husband and life together. Complaining about his refusal to serve Christ or his shortcomings as a man will do nothing but make things worse. It's like telling a child they are bad all the time. Eventually they believe it and begin to go out of their way to act out. They figure, "Mom says I'm bad anyway, so I may as well go ahead and do what I know is wrong." Your husband could take on the same attitude and prove your statements to be true. What happens is, the negative words spoken out of your mouth and others now have life. Words have the ability to bring forth curses or blessings.

You want to always speak blessings and life into every person, place and situation. As children of God and co-heirs with Christ, we have the same power that God used to raise Jesus up from the dead on the inside of us. That's right, we have resurrection power. Keep speaking life into your husband and praying the word of God over his life. It may take a while, but in God's timing, along with your faith, you will see a change.

3

DIVORCED

"...he has sent me to bind up the brokenhearted..."
(Isaiah 61:1 KJV)

Shattered but not broken...

Divorce: the legal dissolution of marriage. A complete or radical separation of closely connected things. To cut off, separate or disunite.

Ever since God established the institution of marriage, the enemy has been trying to destroy it, one way or another. When a man and a woman unite in marriage, they become one in the sight of God. You may have two separate bodies, but your spirits become linked. I imagine it as your souls being sewn together with this eternal needle and thread that cannot be broken by anything in the natural.

A Work in Progress

So when those same two people make the decision to separate by way of divorce, there is a tearing or a ripping, so to speak, of the two souls. It has to be ripped apart because marriage is a spiritual act, a covenant, which is not easily broken. When something is ripped, it usually does a lot of damage, leaving the item in a state of bruised and brokenness.

After the separation of the two souls occurs, there is a rebuilding, healing and forgiveness process that has to take place in order to become whole again. There are many different emotional stages that you may go through during the course of a divorce. Not to mention the changes you go through leading up to that decision. A divorce is similar to a natural death, only without a burial. You may experience a broken heart, anger, rejection, resentment (which can turn into bitterness), guilt, fear and grief. It is natural to feel those things as you are only human, but it is how long you allow yourself to wallow in those emotions that makes the difference. If these feelings are left to fester, they can turn into emotional wounds that make it hard for you to love again. Harboring these types of emotions will also cause you to walk in unforgiveness, which is not pleasing to God.

From your point of view, you are well within your right to be angry, and I am sure others would side with you, but allowing anger to rule your life can be hazardous to your health. Anger has been linked to health issues such as heart attacks, strokes, high blood pressure, anxiety, depression, insomnia and headaches. Harboring anger does nothing but hurt you. The other person may feel your wrath if you decide to act on it, but after that you are the only one it is eating away at. There was a time that I walked around mad at my ex just about every day. Every time I thought about the past situation I would get mad. All of the emotions and feelings I had when we went through our break up would come rushing back, and I would be a mess for the rest of the day. But do you know what he was doing while I was walking around mad? Enjoying his life, not thinking about me. That's right, I was wasting time and energy on someone whose mind I probably hardly ever crossed. It wasn't until I made the decision that I wanted to keep the joy that God had so graciously given me and stop allowing the enemy to steal it by way of past memories that I began to truly live again.

Jesus came that we may have life and life more abundantly (John 10:10). Abundance is defined as a great or plentiful amount; fullness to overflowing; affluence, wealth. A life of abundance is totally opposite from one that is bitter and angry. To paint a picture of the unabundant life, check out (Genesis 1:2). It says that the earth was dark, void and without form.

A Work in Progress

That equates to a bunch of nothing! Your life would be empty because you have given all that you had to someone who left and moved on with their life. You have given all of your energy, time, joy, peace and love to them, and now you have nothing left for yourself. Your life would be a picture of darkness, maybe with hints of light. The Light represents the places where God was trying to come in, but you, being filled with such bile, rejected the Light (Jesus), just as that man rejected you (John 1:5). Whatever reasons were given or whatever situation arose that caused you two to separate has left you feeling angry, sad, useless, unworthy, unloved or unlovable, used, violated, hurt, broken (heart and/or spirit), scattered, lost, scared or anything that is not of God—because every good and perfect gift comes from above (James 1:17). All of those feelings and emotions stem from rejection and abandonment.

To reject something or someone means to refuse to accept or admit, to throw out as useless or worthless, discard. This is usually how a woman feels when a man walks out on her, cheats on her, tells her he doesn't love her anymore, or that he is in love with and leaving her for someone else. After the initial shock wears off, you have to begin to repair the damage that was done to your heart. You are going to need help, and that is where your faith comes in. Jesus came to heal the brokenhearted (Luke 4:18). At one point in my life, my heart was shattered in what felt like a million pieces by a man that I had given all that I had and then some. I knew that the brokenness I felt could only be healed by God, so I picked up the pieces of my heart off the floor and went looking for my Healer. It took a few times of me giving God my heart and taking it back, only to give it back to Him again, before I came to the conclusion that the only way I would truly be healed once and for all was to give it all over to Him and trust God to heal and restore all that had been broken and lost.

Trying to do it on your own is impossible. Sometimes you have to ask God to place forgiveness in your heart. It came to the point that I had to ask that because with all my trying, I still had unforgiveness towards my ex. I would get to a place where I was doing good. Not crying as much, putting everything behind me, moving on, and then the next thing you know, BAM! Grief would come and slap me in the face, and I'd be breaking down out of nowhere over the loss of our relationship. For a long time I could not figure out why these emotions kept resurrecting until a minister told me about soul ties one day. You can make the decision to forgive so that you can move on, but it's the soul ties that need to be severed in order for you to truly go on with your life.

A Work in Progress

A soul tie is the knitting together of two souls that can either bring tremendous blessings in a Godly relationship or tremendous destruction when made with the wrong persons. A soul tie in the Bible can be described not only by the word *knit*, but also by the word *cleave*, which means to bring close together, follow close after, be attached to someone, or adhere to one another as with glue.

You have Godly soul ties (as shown between Johnathan and David in 1 Samuel 18) and ungodly soul ties (as shown in Genesis 34 between Shechem and Dinah). You are tied to friends, parents, siblings, children, your husband, and anyone you have become 'one' (had sex) with. When an ungodly soul tie occurs, you begin to take on their character traits and ones that they have acquired from others. If they are having issues with depression or anger, do not be surprised if you find yourself battling these same issues. All ungodly soul ties must be severed in order to move on in freedom and peace. That is why you must recognize why a person has been placed in your life and who has sent them. Some people are sent because they are needed in your life to get you to your destiny, and some are there to block you from your destiny.

When severing soul ties, you must first repent of any unforgiveness. Next, you must renounce any and all soul ties with that person and/or any other persons you wish to be free from. Call them by name and release their soul back to them. Then, you must cut off all idle communication with them. For example, if you have children, make all communication be only about things pertaining to the children and nothing more. Otherwise, you need time away from them in every way.

Return or get rid of items that person has given you: old letters, stuffed animals, clothing, etc. In some cases, such as family photos, you may want to keep packed away for your children when they get older. You must cut as many ties as possible, both spiritually and naturally. Pray daily for your strength to focus on God and the healing taking place in your heart. With God, ALL things are possible.

4

UNMARRIED WOMEN

*"He who finds a wife finds a good thing,
And obtains favor from the Lord" (Proverbs 18:22 NKJV)*

The scripture listed above is a favorite amongst women. I want to take a closer look at this scripture for you. It says, *"He who finds..."* First off, are you *looking* or *waiting* to be found? A wife is found. She is not out searching for the 'ONE'. As a woman in waiting, you are to be concerning yourself with the things of God (1 Corinthians 7:34). Dr. Maya Angelou said it best, "A woman's heart should be so hidden in God that a man has to seek Him just to find her." The Bible says that if you, *"Delight thyself also in the* LORD: *and he shall give thee the desires of thine heart"* (Psalms 37:4).

A Work in Progress

As you do the work of God, keep His commands and allow the Holy Spirit to lead you and you will be led at the appointed time to cross paths with your God ordained husband.

*"He who finds **a wife**..."* Wife can be defined as the female counterpart in a marital union or covenant. There is more to being a wife than cooking, cleaning, rearing children and providing sexual gratification. Those qualities are good to have as they are an asset to your relationship, but let's go deeper than that. As a single woman who is dedicating her life to Christ while she is waiting on her God ordained husband, God will begin to prepare her. He knows exactly what your husband needs in a wife, so He will begin to purge and purify you of your past baggage.

There will be some things that you will need to be delivered from, curses that may need to be broken off of you, soul ties severed, mind renewed and faith established or refreshed. God will not give His child (your future husband) a product that needs to be remodeled. Not saying that every single issue you have will be resolved, because we are all a work in progress, but you will not be in a broken state falling apart. There are some things in your life that can only be healed and restored by the man designed especially for you.

Ashley Smith

As you are being purged and begin to consecrate yourself before the Lord, He is shaping and molding you, rebuilding you from the ground up. He is taking you in your broken state because, remember, in order to be rebuilt, remade or remodeled you must first be BROKEN. Your foundation is being restored.

Everything the enemy stole from you is being returned. If you lost your identity, God is teaching you who you were designed to be. As women, we often lose ourselves in our relationships, so much so that when that relationship has run its course, we are often left not knowing who we are anymore. We give so much of ourselves away and most of the time to a man who is not even worth it. And the fact that he was not the man God chose for you, he is and was not worth it. The Lord will not only give you back every one of those missing pieces, but He will strengthen you as you receive revelation through His word.

God wants you to be in relationship with Him. He wants you to spend time getting to know Him like you did the man you were interested in. When you are dating, you want to know a man's likes and dislikes. You want to know his interests, what makes him smile, what makes him angry, his goals and aspirations. You want to please him. Have you stopped today and asked God, "What can I do for you today?" or "Lord, teach me

A Work in Progress

to love what you love and hate what you hate so that my life may be pleasing in your sight." When we begin to seek God like we do a man, He will bless us with a man who will exceed our greatest imagination.

We have the ability to adapt to our situation and most times do so out of fear of losing love. God wants you to get to a place of knowing that He is love and He's all you need. He wants you to depend on Him to fulfill your every need. God wants us to have that child-like faith in Him. More like that toddler that depends on her parents to provide her every need, even when she doesn't know how to open her mouth and form the words to ask. I know it is easier said than done, and there have been plenty of times in the past when I would say, "Lord I trust you, I have faith in You." As much as I believed that in my head, I could not get my heart to believe it as well. I was doubtful. Of course I knew that God would never leave me nor forsake me (Hebrews 13:5), and that He would supply my every need according to His riches and glory in Christ Jesus (Philippians 4:19). I read it in His word and I knew that God was not a liar (Numbers 23:19). It took me seeking God wholeheartedly for revelation of His love for me to erase any doubt I had and totally transform my mind.

"He who finds a wife, finds **a good thing and obtains favor with the Lord.**" When first read, it may be interpreted as: I am a good thing and when God sends a man to "find" me, he will be receiving favor. But will he really? Are you a good thing? Are you a wife? Yes, as God formed the Earth and everything on it, He saw that it was good and called it so. But I'm asking, when it comes to becoming a man's wife, are you an asset (good thing) or a liability (bad thing)? An asset is defined as a useful or valuable quality, person, or thing; an advantage or resource. You bring out the best in each other. A liability is something that holds one back; it's a handicap. You don't want to be a hindrance. As a wife, you are to enhance your husbands' life. When you enhance something, you bring value, beauty and effectiveness to it, you enlarge it, and make it greater than it was before. You will be the reflection of your husband. He may appear one way to the world, but who he really is in his heart of hearts will be told by you and your attitude towards life and others.

One thing that I have come to learn about being a woman is that we are moved by love. We were also created to receive love and then give it. You can kind of relate us to the moon. The moon doesn't have its own light; it reflects light off of the sun. And yes, women are natural nurturers and lovers, but a woman reflects what she is given. If she is given love, she will show love. If she is given dirt and water, she will turn around and give someone mud.

A Work in Progress

Let's take a look at the fourth chapter of John: Jesus talks to the Samaritan woman. This unnamed woman was at Jacob's well at the noon hour, the hottest time of day, after the other towns' women had already came and went. She went at that odd time because she was looked down on because of her reputation. As revealed by Jesus, she had had five husbands or had slept with five men and the one she was with now was not her husband. She was the classic example of a woman looking for love in all the wrong places. She was on her sixth man, and it was obvious that she was craving love.

As she stood there talking to Jesus, He told her all about her past and current relationship(s). He saw that she was really in need of a lot more than natural water. She needed the Living Water from a well that will never run dry. She needed to be filled with the love of the Father. This woman needed a full revelation of God's love for her. She was having a personal encounter with the Lover of her soul and didn't even know it. God is saying:

"My precious daughters, I love you all so much. Not only did I give my Son for you but I marked you with my love. That is why if you don't know Me you search relentlessly for that which you believe is missing. Look inside your heart, that is where I am. All the love you need is in Me and I am inside of you. I created you in My

image and in My likeness. The world doesn't have what you need. I am all you need. You are precious. You are priceless. You are royalty. The daughter of THEE King. Come after Me. I have all that you need."

5

SINGLENESS

SINGLE, SAVED & DATING

One subject that continuously comes up when talking with single or unmarried women is dating while saved. Many times that area is neglected in the church while the married relationship is catered to. You often get the "just wait on the Lord" phrase. From my experience, sitting around waiting on anything to fall in your lap gets you nowhere. Faith without works is dead. Not saying that you have to be out, "working" (looking/advertising) for a mate.

A word of wisdom, "He who finds a wife finds a good thing; she who finds a husband finds trouble." Keeping yourself busy with the things of God, improving and carrying yourself as a wife, praying for your future husband even before you meet, and being in the right place at the right time is how you put your faith to work.

The part about being in the right place at the right time means being in the perfect will of God. Being in His will also means knowing what season you are in. Is this your season of waiting/hiding yourself in the Lord? There are different seasons we go through as God reconstructs us. We go through the breaking, the making and the preparation in which we are usually hidden before finally being released to emerge.

The first thing you want to be sure of is that the man is truly saved. (Luke 6:43 KJV) says, *"For a good tree bringeth not forth corrupt fruit; neither doth a corrupt tree bring forth good fruit."* Take time to examine his fruit. The fruit will reveal the type of tree (man) you are dealing with. Also, during that examination process, be sure to go to God in prayer concerning him. Has this man truly been converted, or is he just putting on a façade to win you over?

Don't look for perfection. Does he have a heart that is truly after the heart and not the hand of our Father God? You have to really tune into the Holy Spirit and seek the face of God, blocking out all other voices including your own. Quiet down your desires and opinions of this person and listen to what the Lord is saying. Seeking wise counsel would not be a bad thing to do either if you are having trouble clearly hearing from God, especially if he is someone with whom you are not very familiar with. God will definitely be speaking to you about the man, but it is up to you if you want to take heed to the signs or ignore them.

Trust the Holy Spirit of God inside of you to give you insight concerning the man. In my past, God has used people, situations and had the Holy Spirit tugging at me to get me to see the truth of a man. There will be an unsettling in your spirit. It wasn't until I cut things off with a man that I had begun dating, after my children's father, and accepted the fact that he was a counterfeit that I found complete peace.

Examining his fruit may take time so don't rush it. It may take a few months of being around a person to really get to see their real self emerge. It is easy to mask your true self at the beginning, but you can only do that for so long before the real you begins to come out. Also, it is best to keep as many people out of your business as you get to know this man. Too many people knowing can cause unneeded pressure. You may begin to get lots of unsought advice, and that can cause confusion when seeking God's confirmation of this man in your life.

One of the first things you want to find out when getting to know a man is if he knows his purpose in life. Does he have a God given vision for his future? If yes,

A Work in Progress

then is he fulfilling or taking steps to fulfill his purpose? What is he doing to see the vision come to pass in his life? If the answer is no, he is not ready for a relationship, much less a marriage union. *"Where there is no vision, the people perish"* Proverbs 29:18. If you don't know where they are taking you, don't follow them. Also, it is not your job to hold his hand and teach him how to plan out his life. Let me remind you of a few things: When God presented Eve to Adam, he was in the presence of God (Eden), he had his OWN home (the Garden of Eden), a job (tend to the Garden, Genesis 2:15 NIV). (*"The Lord God took the man and put him in the Garden of Eden to work it and take care of it."*), and a purpose (Genesis 1:28 KJV). (*"And God blessed them, and God said unto them, Be fruitful, and multiply, replenish the earth, and subdue it: and have DOMINION over the fish of the sea and over the fowl in the air and over every living thing that moveth upon the earth."*). If he has not obtained these things, he is not capable of caring for you in the way that you are supposed to be. He is not ready for the ministry of marriage because that is exactly what marriage is—a ministry, a kingdom assignment. A man and a woman are brought together to fulfill the will of God on the earth and bring glory to His name.

After you have confirmed him with God, it is then okay to move forward with your courtship. Courting is the period in a couple's relationship which precedes their engagement and marriage, or establishment of an agreed relationship of a more enduring kind. During courtship, a couple gets to know each other and decide if there will be an engagement or other such agreement.

Courting is dating with a purpose. As you get to know each other, get acquainted with his family and friends. They can help you to see the complete person. Do note that the only perfect man to ever walk the earth was Jesus Christ, so please don't expect him to be perfect. *We are all a work in progress*. No matter what, keep building upon the foundation of Jesus Christ.

Remain pure. Be sure to know your limits and boundaries. Do not allow yourself to be put in the position to be tempted to sin. Even though you are both saved and have been transformed by the renewing of your mind, your flesh has not. It is still the same old flesh. It likes to be pleased, so if you have to set a curfew, do so. For example: No hanging out alone at each other's home after 10 p.m. or no French kissing. For some, that is extreme, but for others that is exactly what it takes to keep them pure and holy. Be true to yourself and do what you have to do to remain that virtuous woman.

A Work in Progress

Once an agreement (engagement) has happened, it is always advisable to seek pre-marital counseling. Counseling can help prepare you both to handle situations that may come up that maybe you weren't anticipating and discuss those things that you may or may not have considered. Marriage success takes two committed people who refuse to give up. If you have not reached this season in your life, do not be discouraged. Continue to trust God and serve Him with your whole heart. Cover your future mate in prayer regularly. Stay at the feet of the master as Mary did in (Luke 10:38-42); He will guide you and keep you as long as you want to be kept.

The most important thing is to be who God has called you to be. It is in that place that you may stumble upon your Boaz as Ruth did. The single season of your life is a time for process and preparation, and cannot be rushed. It all has to happen in God's appointed time. Esther went through a year of purification before she was allowed to be presented before the king. This process can apply to that of preparation of marriage or ministry.

Be anxious for nothing. When the time comes you will be released, be content knowing that you are *A Work In Progress*.

6

WORDS OF WISDOM

This section contains words of wisdom from Christian women across the U.S. and beyond that I petitioned for insight and wisdom concerning marriage, divorce and singleness. I pray these words help guide you as you go through the process of being transformed from "Ashes 2 Life" and continue to be *A Work In Progress*.

1.   *Wait for God.*

– **Anonymous**, Divorcee

2.   *Persevere. Life is hard. God is good.*

– **Mackenzie**, wife of 4 years

A Work in Progress

3. *Wait on God to send you the right mate. When you meet someone you feel is right, allow God to give you the confirmation you need BEFORE you jump the gun and make it what it is not meant to be. A lot of people get married for all the wrong reasons, and GOD did not put them together. IF that is the case then asking GOD for guidance is the first step towards making your marriage what it should be.*

– **Minister Anita Bass**, wife of 19 years

4. *My advice to the unmarried is to pray for the spirit of discernment, that you are guided to your rightful mate. Make sure that you are already balanced and not looking for someone to give you something that they don't have to give. Know your own needs; work out your frailties before looking for a mate.*

– **Mz. Gloria**, wife of 43 years

5. *Patience is needed in any relationship and most importantly in a marriage. Many marriages go through times of trouble, but that is not the time to turn around and walk away. Compromise is definitely a must in all relationships. Be slow to speak but eager to listen. Most importantly, a spiritual foundation*

is the best basic component in relationships. Do not be unequally yoked with a mate/partner. Strong communication skills are a plus as well.

– **L. Ford**, wife of 11 years

6. *Ensure you understand commitment is not about comfort but about being called to fulfill the purpose God has for your life.*

– **Nikki**, wife of 11 years

7. *I would encourage single women to stay single for as long as it takes you until you can become whole and complete in God, being submissive to Him and His instructions, knowing His voice completely. Once you are obedient and submissive to God, you would be that Proverbs 31 woman God has called you to be for your husband. Most importantly, have a forgiving heart in ALL things, destroying ALL bitterness!*

– **Anonymous**, wife of four years

8. *Be consistent as an intercessor for your house. Consistency is key. Acknowledge God in all your ways and He will direct your ways in the wisdom of Christ. Call those things that be not as though they are concerning yourself and your*

family. A righteous woman builds her house, but a foolish one tears hers down.

Get a clear vision of your husband's God-given vision, and do everything you can to bring it to pass. Don't take over the vision, but be that tool that's needed to bring it to pass. Never look at your husband's vision as just his vision. Look at it as the vision for the whole family, because it is God given.

– **Apostle**, wife of 18 years

9. *When you say I do, it means you are in this together. Respect your husband and do not talk down on him. Keep your marriage life private; your problems do not need to be broadcasted. There is always room for reconciliation.*

– **Mrs. DCB**, wife of 22 years

10. *Prepare yourself. If you want to be treated a certain way, make sure you treat your potential mate the same. If you have certain things that annoy people, chances are it will annoy your future mate as well. Make sure you have the best hygiene and be respectful. Have goals of your own and be your own person. Don't lose*

your individuality! That is the mistake many women make.

– **Ms. S**, Divorcee

11. *Love yourself and live it up 'til that day comes to be united with your mate.*

– **Mz. Pplz**, Divorcee

12. *Know who you are before getting married, love yourself first, and remember you are the key to your happiness.*

– **Anonymous**, Divorcee

13. *If you are a Christian, don't even DATE a non-Christian, especially if you seek to honor Jesus Christ as your Lord as well as your Savior. You'll be Satan's target for sure! He will go out of his way to tempt you into sexual sin. Don't date a non-Christian with the thought, "I'll lead him to Christ." It is NOT your role to convert him; that's the Holy Spirit's responsibility!*

And even if he SAYS he's a Christian, DON'T take it for granted that he fully understands what being a Christian means. I thought my fiancé was a Christian because he was a lay-preacher in his denomination. It was only after

> *we married that I realized that he did not have a personal relationship with Jesus.*
>
> – **Ruth**, widowed

ABOUT THE AUTHOR

Ashley Smith's mission is to help others turn their ashes into life by breathing the word of God into every situation and occasion, and sharing the love of Jesus Christ. Though baptized at the age of 11, it wasn't until she was 26 that she formed a personal relationship with Him. Within that connection, she blossomed into the virtuous woman she is today.

She fulfills her passion of helping others achieve their goals as the founder of Ashes 2 Life, LLC, specializing in digital photography, and as an independent myEcon

A Work in Progress

Financial Freedom Expert, teaching people how to achieve financial success.

Ashley currently resides in Junction City, Kansas with her two sons, Anthony and Va'Sean. And when she isn't wearing her business hat, she enjoys worshipping God, singing, traveling, reading, cooking and trying new things.

>   To learn more, be sure to visit:
>   www.about.me/Ashes2Life

WE WANT TO HEAR FROM YOU!!!

If this book has made a difference in your life Ashley would be delighted to hear about it.

Leave a review on Amazon.com!

BOOK ASHLEY TO SPEAK AT YOUR NEXT EVENT!

Send an email to booking@publishyourgift.com

Learn more about Ashley at
www.about.me/Ashes2Life

FOLLOW ASHLEY ON SOCIAL MEDIA

 @Ash2Life   **f** /AuthorAshleySmith

"EMPOWERING YOU TO IMPACT GENERATIONS"
WWW.PUBLISHYOURGIFT.COM

www.ingramcontent.com/pod-product-compliance
Lightning Source LLC
Chambersburg PA
CBHW071537080526
44588CB00011B/1709